ADVENTURE TIME

with

Fionna & Cake
CARD WARS

ADVENTURE TIME™ WITH FIONNA AND CAKE: CARD WARS.
ISBN: 9781785853258
Published by Titan Comics, a division of Titan Publishing Group Ltd.,
144 Southwark St., London, SE1 0UP. Contains material originally
published in single comic form as ADVENTURE TIME FIONNA AND
CAKE CARD WARS 1-6. © Cartoon Network (S16) All rights reserved.
ADVENTURE TIME, CARTOON NETWORK, the logos, and all related
characters and elements are trademarks of and © Cartoon Network.
All characters, events and institutions depicted herein are fictional. Any
similarity between any of the names, characters, persons, events and/or
institutions in this publication to actual names, characters, and persons,
whether living or dead and/or institutions are unintended and purely
coincidental. TCN 1776

A CIP catalogue record for this title is available from the British Library.

Printed in China.

10 9 8 7 6 5 4 3 2 1

ADVENTURE TIME™ created by
PENDLETON WARD

written by JEN WANG

CHAPTER ONE
illustrated by BRITT WILSON

CHAPTERS TWO-SIX
pencils and letters by BRITT WILSON
inks and colours by RIAN SYGH

cover by JEN WANG

with special thanks to
MARISA MARIONAKIS, RICK BLANCO,
CURTIS LELASH, CONRAD MONTGOMERY,
NICOLE RIVERA, MEGHAN BRADLEY,
KELLY CREWS, SCOTT MALCHUS,
ADAM MUTO AND THE WONDERFUL
FOLKS AT CARTNOON NETWORK

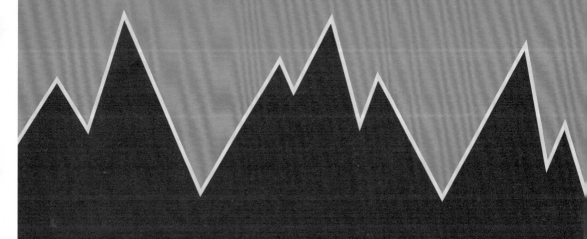

chapter one

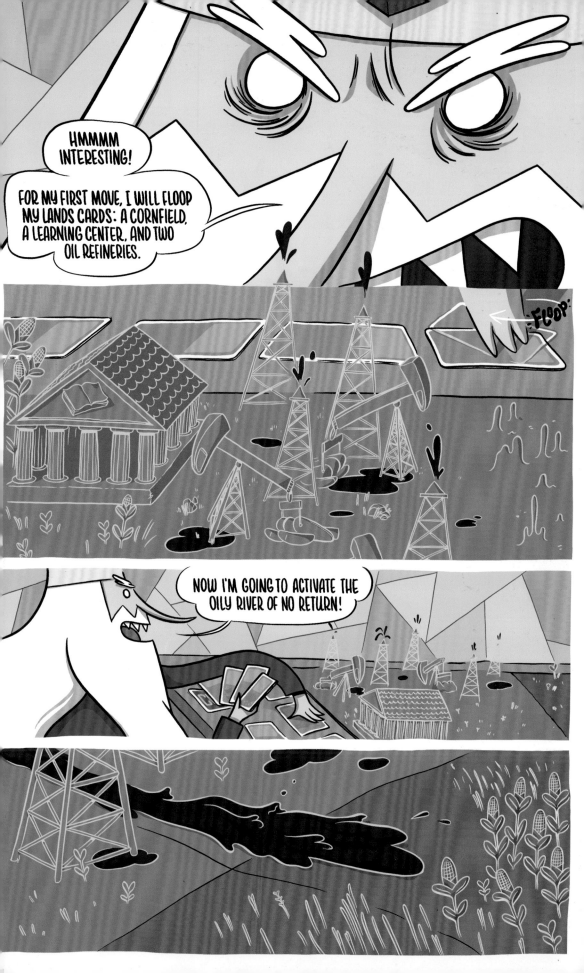

CUTE?? FIONNA, YOU GOTTA START PLAYING MORE STRATEGICALLY.

I KNOW, I JUST LIKE THE CARDS THAT LOOK NICE.

WELL, ALRIGHT. DON'T SAY I DIDN'T WARN YA.

DON'T WORRY LONELY PANDA. I BELIEVE IN YOU. ATTACK!

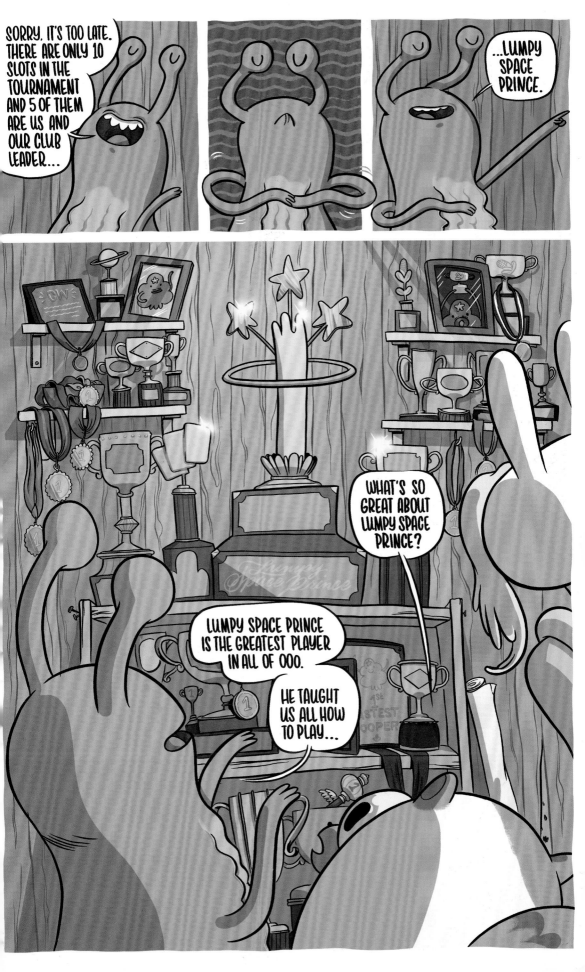

Lumpy Space Prince!

OH!

WHUMP

chapter two

THANK YOU, M'DEAR.

ARE YOU GOING TO BE OKAY, LUMPY SPACE PRINCE?

WHAT HAPPENED?

SIGH I'LL BE ALRIGHT, WALLY. IT STARTED WHEN THE OFFICIAL TOURNAMENT PLAYERS WERE ANNOUNCED...

NONE OF US HAD EVER EVEN HEARD OF THIS PLAYER BEFORE SO OF COURSE THE IDEA HE WAS CALLING HIMSELF A "MASTER" WAS PREPOSTEROUS.
WHEN HE MENTIONED HE WAS WILLING TO PRACTICE WITH US, I TOOK HIM UP ON HIS OFFER. MAYBE I COULD SHOW HIM A THING OR TWO, TEACH HIM SOME HUMILITY.

NOW THE TOURNAMENT MUST GO ON WITHOUT ME.

LSP, NO!

weep sob weep cry

I'M SORRY, MY FRIENDS. I'M SORRY I HAVE FAILED YOU ALL.

HMPH! THIS **FLOOP MASTER** THINKS HE CAN SCARE US. HE CAN'T EVEN SHOW HIS FACE!

BUT I AM SCARED!

I'M NOT. I'LL TAKE ON THE FLOOP MASTER.

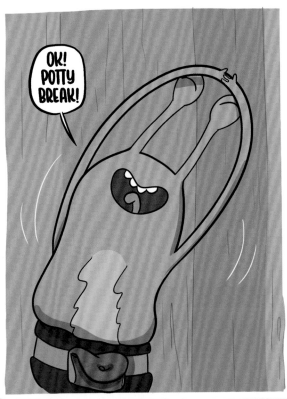

SOMETHING YOU WOULD LEAST SUSPECT.

HOW IS THAT?

WALLY ONLY KNOWS HOW TO PLAY AGGRESSIVELY. HE USES CARDS THAT INFLICT THE MOST DAMAGE, BUT HE SPENDS LITTLE TIME GUARDING HIS DEFENSES.

WHY ARE YOU TELLING ME THIS?

BECAUSE YOU REMIND ME OF ME. YOU'RE SMART AND I THINK YOU HAVE WHAT IT TAKES TO DEFEAT THE FLOOP MASTER.

THANKS.

NOD

GOOD LUCK.

READY TO GET BACK?

LET'S GO!

THE NAKED MOLE RAT?? GOOD GRIEF, ARE YOU SURE YOU'VE PLAYED THIS GAME BEFORE?

I FLOOP MY GREAT WALL OF SILENCE AND ACTIVATE MY NAKED MOLE RAT!

chapter three

I DON'T THINK CARD WARS IS APPROPRIATE FOR BABIES. WE'LL HOLD ON TO THESE FOR YOU UNTIL YOU'RE OLDER.

HEY! THOSE ARE MINE! I BOUGHT THOSE WITH MY ALLOWANCE MONEY!

OOPS!

YOU'RE BEING A GOOD FRIEND! THIS TOURNAMENT IS VERY IMPORTANT TO CAKE.

WWISHING WELLLLL! DON'T MISS THE WISHING WELLL

WISHING WELL

OOH!

SORRY.

NO LONE WISHERS.

WHAT! AAAAW.

PIE CATAPULT! COME TRY THE PIE CATAPULT!

THE BIG CARD WARS CHAMPIONSHIP. IT'S HER **DREAM!** I'M HAPPY FOR HER, I JUST WISH I WERE A PART OF IT.

DON'T WORRY, FIONNA. THINGS WILL WORK OUT. I HAVE A FEELING THEY WILL.

chapter four

BE NICE, CAKE

OH!

FIONNA!

PRINCE GUMBALL! WHAT ARE *YOU* DOING HERE?

I'M HERE TO WATCH THE CARD WARS TOURNAMENT!

BEING MESSY IS UNACCEPTABLE

I'M THE ROYAL SPONSOR!

SPONSORED BY THE CANDY KINGDOM

OF COURSE IT IS. IT'S THE ONLY THING THAT'S IMPORTANT ANYMORE.

THIS IS FOR YOU.

SEE YOU AFTER THE TOURNAMENT.

ALL PLAYERS PREPARE TO ENTER THE STADIUM!

AW FIONNA, C'MON!

COME ON, CAKE! WE GOTTA GO!

GOOOOOO CHAMPIONS!

Floop

VICTORY: CAKE!
VICTORY: CAKE!
VICTORY: CAKE!
VICTORY: CAKE!
WELL WELL, I HAVEN'T SEEN YOU HERE BEFORE.

WELL, I HAVEN'T HEARD THAT ONE BEFORE, BUT SURE, I'LL TAKE IT.

RIFFLE

FLIFF

FWOP

FWIP

FWAP

READY WHEN YOU ARE.

SIT.

TOSS

AWWW.

PIZZA!

chapter five

LSP, WHAT AM I GOING TO DO? THE GAME'S BARELY STARTED AND I'M A MESS! LOOK AT ME!

HEH HEH HEH HEH HEH

SHUFFLE

NOT TO RUSH YOU, BUT THE SOONER YOU CAN GO HOME, THE SOONER YOU CAN NURSE THAT WRIST!

GRRRR!!

LISTEN, WHO'S THE BEST PLAYER HERE?

UH... THE FLOOP MASTER?

WHAP!

OH, FIONNA, I'M SO SORRY. YOU'RE THE ONE WHO HAD FAITH IN ME ALL ALONG.

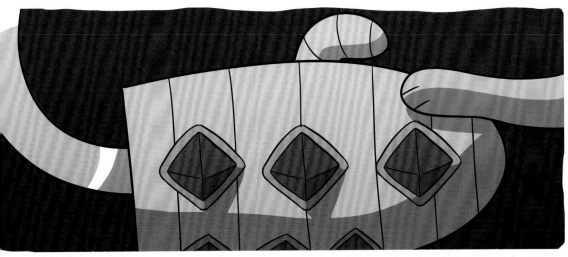

SNIFFLE

HUH?

I SHOULD BE GETTING BACK INSIDE. THEY MUST BE FINISHING UP. SEE YOU LATER, FIONNA!

SWISH

OH NO, CAKE...!

I ABSORB ALL MY ARMIES INTO THE CACTUS CAVALRY AND MOVE THEM TO THE FRONTLINES.

HUP!

Getting Comfy

YOUR MOVE.

WAIT! BUT I JUST--

IT'S HIM! THE ONE WHO BEAT ME! HE'S THE REAL FLOOP MASTER!

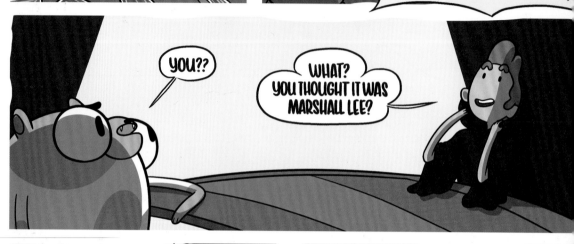

YOU??

WHAT? YOU THOUGHT IT WAS MARSHALL LEE?

SHRUG

FINAL GAME STARTS WITH PLAYER 2-- CAKE!

chapter six

FIRST I ACTIVATE *FOREST OF HAPPY FEELINGS!*

POP

NEXT I FLOOP *LONELY PANDA!*

WHAT?

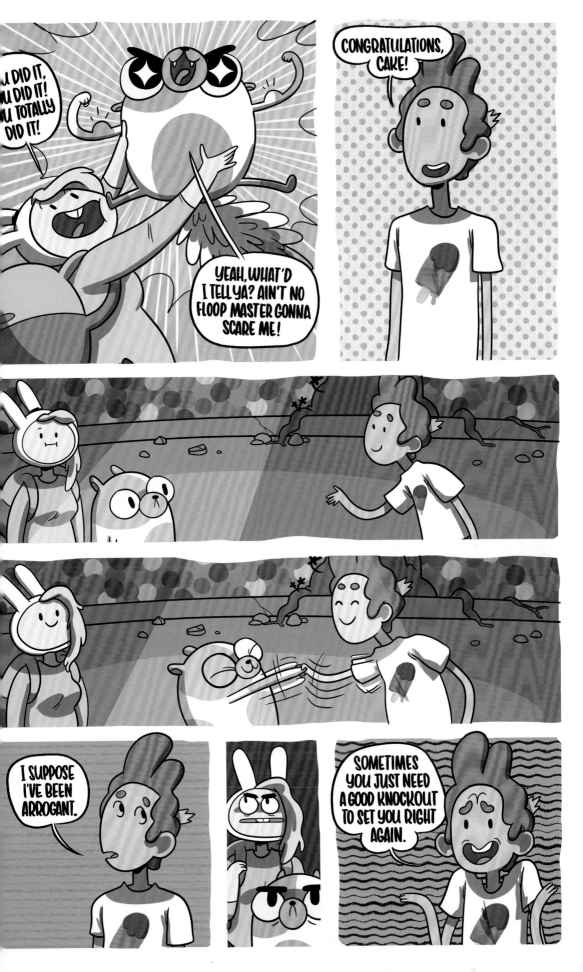

SO.

WHAT TO NEXT?

I DUNNO ABOUT YOU CAKE, BUT I REALLY FEEL LIKE PLAYING ANOTHER ROUND OF CARD WARS...

...WITH THE ICE KING!

HUH??

HE'S ONLY THE MOST HANDSOME, COURAGEOUS, TALENTED...

The End

issue two cover
JEN WANG

issue one subscription
WYETH YATES

issue one variant
JOHN KOVALIC

issue one boom! ten years variant
JEFFREY BROWN

issue one san diego comic-con exclusive
MAD RUPERT

issue one a shop called quest exclusive
JESSIE WONG

issue one diamond san diego comic-con exclusive
MICHELLE CZAJKOWSKI

issue two subscription
NICOLE HAMILTON

issue two variant
MAYA KERN

issue three subscription
WENDI CHEN

issue three variant
DANIELA VIÇOSO

issue four subscription
DANA TERRACE

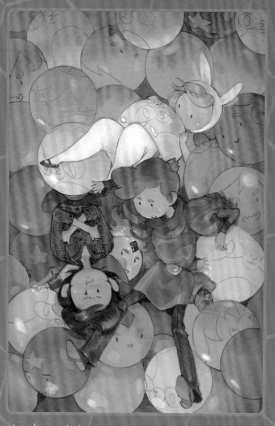

issue four variant
RACHEL SAUNDERS

issue five subscription
MYKEN BOMBERGER

issue five variant
DIANA HUH

issue six subscription
REBEKKA DUNLAP